LOSING A FAMILY MEMBER

MEMORIES

BY HOLLY DUHIG

BookLife
PUBLISHING

©2018
BookLife Publishing
King's Lynn
Norfolk PE30 4LS

All rights reserved.
Printed in Malaysia.

A catalogue record for this book is available from the British Library.

ISBN: 978-1-78637-287-1

Written by:
Holly Duhig

Edited by:
Kirsty Holmes

Designed by:
Danielle Rippengill

All facts, statistics, web addresses and URLs in this book were verified as valid and accurate at time of writing.
No responsibility for any changes to external websites or references can be accepted by either the author or publisher.

Image Credits

All images are courtesy of Shutterstock.com, unless otherwise specified. With thanks to Getty Images, Thinkstock Photo and iStockphoto. Front Cover – Nong Mars, prapann, Alexander Lysenko, Flas100, You Touch Pix of EuToch, tr3gin, Diyana Dimitrova, LesPalenik, Studio ART, Alexandra Lande. Images used on every spread – Red_Spruce, MG Drachal, Alexander Lysenko, Kues, Flas100, Kanate, Mc Satori. 1 – Nong Mars. 2 – Inna_liapko. 4 – India Picture. 5 – Robert Crum. 6 & 7 – India Picture.8 – Alliance, Nikolaeva. 9 – Pammy Studio, TravnikovStudio. 10 – India Picture. 11 – medveda, Nikolaeva. 12 – Elena Dijour. 13 – Lighthunter. 14 – India Picture. 15 – S_Photo. 16 – Xubayr Mayo, Nikolaeva. 17 – India Picture. 18 – WorldWide. 19 – Art Studio, Nikolaeva. 20 – Inna_liapko. 21 – India Picture. 22 & 23 – India Picture.

Contents

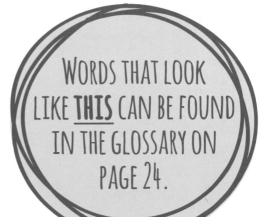

Words that look like **THIS** can be found in the glossary on page 24.

My Family ♡

THIS IS GRANDAD SANJAY.

My name is Amir. I live with my mum, dad, little sister and grandma. My grandad used to live with us too, but he died a while ago.

Grandad lived with us in our house. We have a big house, but sometimes it feels empty without him there.

OUR HOUSE

My Grandad

My grandad was really cool. He looked after me when Mum and Dad were at work, and played video games with me.

My grandad told me lots of stories about what life was like when he was young. He also taught me how to play chess.

As Grandad got older, he became very **forgetful**. It wasn't long before I had to remind him how to play chess.
He also had to visit the hospital more and more.

Before Grandad died, we all went to visit him in the hospital. I gave him Rabbit so she could take care of Grandad while I wasn't there.

RABBIT

Asking Questions ???

When the doctors told us that Grandad was going to die, I didn't really know what they meant. I didn't know what happened when people died.

LUCY

Mum told me that when someone dies, their heart stops beating and their bodies are still. It made me think of our cat, Lucy, who died when I was two.

Mum said all living things die eventually including people. She also said that most people live long, happy lives and die when they are very old.

GRANDAD HAS LOTS OF PHOTOS OF HIS LIFE.

When people have been ill for a long time, dying can be a **PEACEFUL** END.

I was worried that dying would hurt Grandad, but Dad said that people don't feel any pain when they have died.

Feeling Sad 🙁

DAD

GRANDAD

ME

When Grandad died, I cried a lot. So did my dad. Mum said we all needed time to **grieve**. I took some time off school and Dad took time off work.

Mum wanted me to eat but I didn't want to. I missed seeing Grandad at the dinner table. Everything reminded me of him.

THIS USED TO BE GRANDAD'S CHAIR.

FEELING SCARED 😟

Going to sleep made me feel scared. Grandad died in his sleep. What if I didn't wake up, like Grandad?

GRANDMA

Grandma told me that sleeping is not the same as dying. Sleeping is just our bodies taking a rest. Grandad died because he was very old, not because he was sleeping.

After Grandad died, I would have **nightmares.** Sometimes I woke up and I had wet the bed. This made me feel **embarrassed**.

Mum said there was nothing to be embarrassed about, and it's normal to feel scared sometimes.

MUM GAVE ME A DIARY SO I COULD WRITE DOWN MY FEELINGS BEFORE GOING TO BED.

REMEMBERING

WE LIGHT CANDLES TO REMEMBER GRANDAD.

I still miss Grandad, but I don't feel as sad as I used to.
Now I know there are lots of ways you can remember someone.

Remembering someone can be a happy thing.
I helped Grandma make a photo album of Grandad's life.
Some of the photos made us laugh!

MY SISTER LIKES TO LOOK AT THE PHOTOS TOO.

FEELING BETTER

It's been a long time now since Grandad died and I don't think about it as much anymore. This is OK.

Even if I forget little things, I won't forget how much I loved Grandad and how much he loved me.

Glossary and Index

Glossary

embarrassed	to feel awkward, self–conscious or ashamed
eventually	after a while
forgetful	forgetting lots of things, or forgetting easily
grieve	to feel sad after losing a loved one
nightmares	frightening dreams caused by stress
peaceful	free from disturbance or pain

Index

24